This is no ordinary
dream journal.

*This is your book of
transformation.*

the little dream journal

a space to spark insights from
your midnight mind

Tzivia Gover

Smith
Street
Books

I've had such a curious dream.

Lewis Carroll,
Alice's Adventures in Wonderland

contents

WELCOME

to the

LITTLE
DREAM
JOURNAL

Following your dreams is more than just a cliché.
It's a way of life filled with creativity, purpose, and joy.
Your dream journal is where the journey begins.

On these pages, you will not only record your dreams but also tune
into the sage guidance of your midnight mind and bring its wisdom
into the light of day. This everyday magic unfolds when you put pen
to paper and reflect on your dreams and waking experiences.

Writing dreams, even the scary ones, can help you understand them
and yourself more fully. When you make space for dreams on the page,
you make space for your intuitive voice to be heard so you can improve
your relationships at home, work, and in the community—and live
with a sense of increased connection and meaning.

Those might sound like lofty claims but it's just an acknowledgment of the ordinary powers of the dreaming mind. During REM sleep, when most memorable dreams take place, we are primed for learning, problem-solving, insight, emotional regulation, and thinking outside the box. Writing about your dreams is the foundational practice to help you access all these benefits and more.

Whether you are new to keeping a dream journal or have been journaling dreams for years, *The Little Dream Journal* offers easy and effective techniques to help you remember and record dreams so the wellspring of your dreaming mind can nourish you.

And whether you remember dreams nightly, only occasionally, or if you want to remember more dreams, this journal is for you too. Unlike most dream journals, here you will have space to record dreams side by side with reflections on your waking life. Plus, you'll receive tips for engaging with your midnight mind even when you don't remember any dreams.

By picking up this journal, you've taken the first step. You've now given your subconscious mind the message that you are ready to remember and respond to your dreams. And within even a short amount of time writing in it, you will likely begin to recall even more of them. As time goes on, page by page you'll discover that this little journal might just become your book of transformation.

In this journal you will:

- record dreams using a format to help you access their meaning and propel your inner growth

- experience how keeping a dream journal can transform the third of your life you spend asleep into a lifelong adventure of discovery

- make useful associations between waking experiences and dreams

- strengthen your intuition and self-confidence

- and much more.

A quick GUIDE

to your

BOOK *of* TRANSFORMATION

Writing in a dream journal is easy. But if that's *all* you do, you won't receive the full array of gifts available to you, and you're more likely to abandon the project quickly.

That's why this journal provides features designed to maximize the pleasures and perks of journaling so it will become a cherished ritual you look forward to returning to again and again. Keep reading for a quick overview of what you'll find here.

the daily template

This is where you'll record your dreams. The prompts will help you connect with their storehouse of intelligence and information. On days you *don't* remember dreams, use this space to write about thoughts you wake up with, intentions for your day, or anything else on your mind in the morning.

journaling prompts

These sentence starters and journaling suggestions will help you generate dream-inspired writing. Use them in any order and return to your favorites again and again.

long-form pages

Use the lined long-form pages to let your thoughts roam freely or to dig deeper into dreams. Here, you can respond to the journaling prompts and explore associations, observations, thoughts, and questions about your dreams. Or turn your dreams into stories, poems, or other creative expressions.

free-form pages

Use the unlined free-form pages to express yourself artistically. This is a space to draw, paint, or collage your dreams.

quotes and mantras

Interspersed throughout the journal you'll find affirming words to spark your curiosity and inspire you on your journey.

dream index

Use the grid provided to help you organize and track key details about each dream so you can locate a specific dream or identify recurring themes and patterns between dreams.

rules for the (unruly) road

This journal may be beautiful but between its covers you have permission to be messy. After all, creativity blossoms in infinite colors, shapes, and designs. Consider this a judgment-free zone where you can write anything and cross out when you need to. Misspellings are welcome, as are rambling sentences or random fragments.

Each dream is as unique as you are, so make this journal your own! If any of the tips or prompts don't resonate for you, adapt them as needed. Or skip what's not working for you.

midnight writer

If you want to remember dreams, writing them down before you kick off the covers is best. That can mean writing in the dark when you've woken from a dream at 3 a.m. or writing with your journal propped on your knees as your cat competes for space on your lap. Often, you'll find yourself trying to compose sentences before you've had your first cup of coffee. Then there's the challenge of deciphering your half-asleep handwriting later on. These tips can help:

nightstand

Set yourself up for nighttime and pre-dawn writing with a bedside table to store your journal, pens and pencils, and a lamp (preferably with a dimmer switch).

night notes

Along with your journal, it's helpful to keep a pad of scratch paper close at hand. When you wake from a dream at night, use these slips of paper to jot down a few details that will jog your memory in the morning, but not so much description that you'll lose out on sleep. Refer to these notes later when you're ready to spend time with your journal.

light up the page

A light-up pen (yes, that's a thing!) is ideal for writing dreams in the middle of the night. The illuminated tip sheds just enough light to see the page in front of you—but not enough to stun you (and your bed partner if you have one) awake with the glare of a phone light or bedside lamp.

in praise of pencils

Writing dreams in bed can get messy. To prevent ink stains on your pillows and sheets, use a pen with a retractable tip or opt for a pencil. Pencils are also handy when you remember dreams out of sequence, so you can erase and re-arrange lines easily.

dream in color

Keep some colored pencils or markers nearby to highlight intriguing lines, phrases, and images or to sketch a dreamscape. Or just add a random dash of color!

mind your p's

Along with pen and paper, you also need persistence to strengthen the writing habit and *permission* to be imperfect, make mistakes, and be messy. With persistence and permission, you'll develop a writing practice that will serve you for years to come.

*Every one that sleeps
is beautiful,
every thing in the
dim light is beautiful.*

Walt Whitman,
"The Sleepers"

making time

The most common obstacle to keeping a dream journal is time.
But even spending a few minutes on the page goes a long way.
To honor the demands of the clock and still make space for your
dreams, consider these suggestions:

less is more

Prioritize the quality of your time with your dream journal over the
quantity. As dreamers, we value our need for rest.

hit snooze

Set your alarm for ten minutes before you need to get out of bed.
When the alarm goes off, hit the snooze button, and pick up your
dream journal. Ten minutes later, when the alert pings, bring your
writing to a close and get out of bed. Trust that whatever you had time
to write was enough, and you can add more later if you like.

perfectly imperfect

Expecting to remember dreams every day, or pressuring yourself to
write down every one, are both recipes for disappointment. If you
only have time to write a line or two most mornings, you can catch up
with a longer stretch on the weekend. If you skip a day or two, or even
three, just pick up the journal the next chance you get. Give yourself
permission to be imperfect.

precious moments

Create a cozy and comforting journaling practice that is rooted in the
pleasure and satisfaction of connecting with your dreams. When you
value and enjoy the moments with your journal, you'll want to find
more time to spend on the page.

remember why

If it seems like you don't have even five minutes for journaling, it might
be that instead of more time, you need more motivation. List three or
more reasons you *want* to write here. Then re-read your reasons when
you need encouragement to return to these pages. Update your list as
needed—or as new reasons to keep writing arise.

Where
DREAMS

come
from

You've been dreaming since you were floating in the womb, and on average each of us will have had well over 100,000 dreams during a healthy lifespan.

As a species, chances are we've been dreaming at least since humans first evolved. Some archeologists even posit that cave paintings might have included depictions of dreams and visions along with illustrations of daily events. If true, that would make them the first dream journals!

And for as long as we've been dreaming, people have debated what dreams mean and where they come from. Through the ages, they have alternately been hailed as messages from the gods and dismissed as meaningless hallucinations from a mind divorced from reason.

And yet, many indigenous cultures throughout time have valued, and still value, dreams and visions and have developed methods for dream catching and rituals for dream sharing. Most regard dreams as guidance from ancestors, the collective web of knowledge, or spirits whose messages are delivered to benefit individuals and the community.

Mystical and contemplative traditions such as Kabbalah, Sufism, and Tibetan Dream Yoga have contributed to our understanding of dreams and created protocols for dreamwork—many of which have stood the test of time.

Today's understanding of dreaming is still heavily influenced by the contributions of Sigmund Freud and Carl G. Jung and their disciples. Drawing on the scientific understanding of his time, Freud first theorized that dreams are a product of the sleeping brain. Jung popularized the exploration of dream archetypes and the function of the collective unconscious. Together, their work brought dreams to the analyst's couch as well as into public discourse and popular culture.

Then 20th-century science challenged religious and psychological theories and practices by reporting that dreams result from random neuronal firings from the brainstem and have no inherent meaning.

Thanks to today's sophisticated brain imaging technology, we know that when we close our eyes and turn off the lights, our brain is not resting. During REM sleep it is highly active and operates with a different chemical makeup than the mind when it's awake. The dreaming brain is primed for making unusual associations, activating heightened emotions, rich visual imagery, and metaphoric language. This prepares us for outside-the-box thinking to gain new perspectives and solve problems more effectively. It also explains why so many innovations and artistic breakthroughs, from the periodic table to Google, have come from dreams and visions.

Dreaming has also been proven to help us process daily events and emotions, consolidate memory, integrate learning, and prepare us for epiphanies. Dreams may have contributed to human evolution by providing a virtual training ground to test strategies for implementation in waking life.

Because dreams are subjective in nature, science alone may never answer all our questions about dreaming. Even with all the breakthroughs and advances in science and psychology, the formation and function of dreams remain cloaked in some degree of mystery. And what we do know about them is constantly being updated.

That's why approaching dreams with openness to a variety of perspectives including mystical, psychological, and scientific—as well as personal experience—remains the best way to appreciate our dreams' complexity, power, and beauty.

The DREAMER'S TOOLBOX

dream recall

We accept that we remember some things and forget others. But when it comes to dreams, we more or less expect to forget. In fact, exponentially more dreams are forgotten than remembered. Of the three to five dreams we average each night, most people remember only a few each *week*.

Dream recall can be challenging for a variety of reasons. For instance, the brain areas that support short-term memory are less active when we're dreaming. Diminished dream recall may also be a protective adaptation, so we don't confuse dreams with waking experiences. Any number of additional factors can also inhibit dream recall including medications or supplements, stress, and inadequate sleep.

Happily, boosting dream recall is easy. By creating favorable conditions for sleep and writing dreams down, most people can remember more of them. Keep reading for additional ways to enjoy a more bountiful dream harvest.

the write intention

Writing dreams down is a tried and true way to boost recall.
Better yet, seal the intention at bedtime by writing it in your journal:
Tonight, I will remember my dreams. In the morning, record any
dreams including fragments, snippets, or general impressions.
If you don't remember any right away, still pick up your journal and
pen. Something might come to you, and if not, you've signaled to
your subconscious that you are prepared to receive more next time.

stay still

Before you open your eyes in the morning, spend a few moments in
the position you were sleeping in to encourage dream memories to
flow back to you.

write away

Even if you remember a dream when you wake up, it's common to forget
it by the time you sit down for breakfast—unless you write it down.
Even if you don't have time to record the entire dream, take a few notes
to remind yourself when you return to your journal later on.

positive messaging

Negative thoughts and statements can negatively affect your dream
recall. Avoid saying or thinking *I don't remember my dreams.* Instead
try *I'm open to remembering more dreams*, or *I'm building my capacity
to remember my dreams.*

take an interest

To remember more dreams, get curious about dreams, read articles
or books about them, and ask others about their dreams. People who
focus more on dreams and dreaming tend to remember more.

keep the door open for dreams

If you don't remember a dream first thing in the morning, don't give
up. Dream fragments, or even an entire scene, may come to you while
you are taking a shower, walking the dog, or even commuting to work.

Ask your dreams anything.

But be prepared to
wait for the answer.

Tzivia Gover

I don't remember

No dream recall? No worries. Even when you don't remember your dreams, they remember you! You've been dreaming either way, and your dreaming mind is supporting you. Keep setting your intention to remember. In the meantime, you can also try these techniques:

waking dreams

Consider events in your waking life with the same curiosity and wonder that you would apply to dreams.

report it

Use the dream report template to write about something out of the ordinary that occurred during an otherwise ordinary day: for example, you stepped out of a shop to find a deer strolling gracefully along the pavement, or a stranger on the bus offered you a croissant. You can use any of the prompts and techniques offered, such as giving the incident a title, writing in the first person, using present tense, etc. Just tag the entry as a waking dream so you don't get confused later on.

pick a dream

Choose a card at random from your favorite tarot or oracle deck and consider the image on the card as if it were a dream. You can then use any of the prompts or exercises in this journal and relate it to that dreamy image.

dream incubation

While we tend to think dreams are purely random occurrences over which we have no control, the reality is quite different. It is healthy and natural to take steps to influence our dreams, and we do so whether we're aware of it or not. What we eat before bed, what we watch on TV, and what we think and talk about at night all affect the quality and content of our dreams.

But still, some people wonder whether it's okay to request guidance from their dreams, believing that the processes of the subconscious mind should not be tampered with.

It might help to remember that while we can nudge our dreams in a certain direction, they will have the final say if there's something more urgent or compelling to address.

The practice of dream incubation or inviting dreams to help with a particular issue or ailment is an ancient one. There is evidence of sleep and dream temples dating back thousands of years where seekers would undergo rituals to receive messages and healing from gods and goddesses in their dreams.

But there's no need to go on a pilgrimage or learn esoteric practices to incubate a dream. Simply pose a question about something you need intuitive guidance on and write it in your journal. For example:

Tonight in my dreams I'll see what is blocking me.
Show me what I need to know in my life right now for my highest good.
Show me what I need to know or do to improve my health.
Show me what I might experience if I accept this job offer/say yes
to this relationship, etc.

As the examples demonstrate, open-ended suggestions, rather than yes/no questions, work best. Also, because dreams communicate primarily through imagery, use wording such as *Show me ...* or *Tonight I will see ...* in your query. Here are more tips for dream incubation:

- Choose a question or issue that has emotional resonance or importance for you.
- Put a picture or object that represents your question near your bed or under your pillow or mattress to strengthen your intention.
- Journal about the issue or question you're seeking guidance on before bed.
- Write your intention and repeat it one to three times in your mind as you are falling asleep and then again if you wake in the middle of the night.
- Write your dream in the morning and review it for any ways it might connect with your intention.
- Keep an open mind; even if your dream doesn't seem to answer your question at first, have faith that it has. Getting input from a friend or dream group members can help.
- If you don't recall any dreams, write something in your journal anyway, such as: *I woke up feeling ...* or *I woke up thinking about ...* Then try again. It may take several attempts, so be patient.

dream interpretation

There is no one-size-fits-all interpretation for any dream image or symbol. And yet, because we are hungry for answers to the cryptic messages from our midnight mind, we turn to dream dictionaries or type our requests for interpretation into search engines. But no book or algorithm can interpret your dream for you. It's helpful to get input from others, but ultimately, the surest place to find answers is inside yourself.

After all, your dreams are not trying to confound you. In fact, they are speaking in an imagistic and symbolic language whose vocabulary is tailor-made for you, using your own memories and associations. And just by writing dreams down, *aha's* of new understanding might spark within you! Also try:

pull on a thread

When a dream feels like a tangle of confusing elements, choose one word or phrase that elicits curiosity or emotion. Start writing about that part of the dream and see where it leads you. Then pull on another thread, and another, until you weave a little swatch of meaning from it.

give it time

If you are still perplexed after journaling about your dream or talking it over with a friend, let it rest. Over the course of a day, a week, or maybe longer, new insights might arise without much effort on your part.

write by hand

Sure, on your computer, tablet, or phone, your fingers and thumbs can race across the keyboard as you type a dream. But dreamwork isn't a race. So, pick up a pen and stroll through your dream. At that pace you're able to notice the thoughts and feelings that arise as you revisit the experience. Typing dreams and voice recording them have their place. But writing by hand is a uniquely constructive way to connect fully with dreams.

befriend your dream

As you write, listen to your dream the way you'd want to be listened to by your BFF: with patient, curious, and non-judgmental attention. Like your friend, the dream will reveal more when it knows that you are paying attention.

ask, don't tell

It's tempting to impose a cookie-cutter interpretation on a dream. But you'll learn more when you pose open-ended questions (those that don't dead-end into yes/no answers) like, *What does that dream make me think about?* or *How does it make me feel?* and *What might it be trying to tell me?*

no need to understand

There's more to do with a dream than just interpreting it. Begin by appreciating it. Admire the dream's creativity, uniqueness, wit, or narrative prowess. As in life, sometimes the point is simply to enjoy it.

dream action

You may think of a dreamer as someone who has their head in the clouds. But active dreamers take their dreams off the pillow and incorporate the information they receive into their daily life.

You don't have to know what your dream means to activate its power. Honoring your dream in a tangible way, even just writing it down, helps complete the circuit of your nighttime and daytime consciousness to empower your intuition and inner wisdom.

Along with creating an action or affirmation when you write your dream report, there are countless ways to take your dream into the day. Experiment with one or more of these—and add your own:

- Create a mini ritual like lighting a candle, sitting quietly, and contemplating a dream theme or image.
- Place an object or symbol that represents your dream on your desk, bedside table, or altar to remind you of its wisdom.
- Put on music that matches the feeling or theme of your dream and dance to it.
- Wear a color, scarf, tie, or piece of jewelry to remind you of your dream throughout the day.
- Connect with someone who showed up in your dream. If appropriate, phone or message them just to check in and say hello. (It's optional to mention that you saw them in your dream.)
- Plan to make amends or clarify a misunderstanding with someone based on a new perspective gained in a dream. If that's not possible or not a healthy option, you can direct your thoughts to them in a journal entry meant for your eyes only.
- Create a poem, story, or any other form of artistic expression from your dream to honor or celebrate it.

Go gently. Simple actions that spark more peace, creativity, joy, and love in your life (and certainly do no harm) are ideal. Start small. Then observe whether new dreams or events confirm—or offer a course correction to—the direction you are moving in.

Let me not mar that
perfect dream

By an auroral stain,

But so adjust my
daily night

That it will come again.

Emily Dickinson

Re-Balancing Act

Troubleshooting
COMMON
DREAM ISSUES

Dream journaling is usually beneficial and deeply satisfying. But sometimes remembering and recording dreams can be inconvenient, uncomfortable, or even disquieting. That's because when we open ourselves to dreams, we open the doors to the subconscious mind.

In that vast and subterranean realm, we encounter memories that we may have suppressed or avoided for a long time. Revisiting them can feel overwhelming. In most cases, small shifts, like the ones that follow, can help.

so many dreams, so little time

Remembering more dreams is usually a welcome development. But if you start to remember so many that writing them down is taking too much time, if abundant recall becomes a distraction, or if it interferes with your sleep, make some adjustments:

fine-tune the flow

You can take a few days off from writing dreams or decide only to write down particularly impactful dreams to suppress dream recall temporarily. Then when you're ready for more, go back to writing more dreams down.

wait and see

If you have vivid dream recall, and don't have time to write it all down, wait a few hours to pick up your journal. Some details will be lost, but you'll likely remember what's most important. And if you missed something crucial, it's likely to show up in another dream later on.

request less

Just as you can set an intention to remember more dreams, you can also ask for just "one clear dream," or even a night of dreamless sleep. You might be surprised at how responsive your dreaming mind can be.

a cure for dream hangovers

If a dream is so intense that you can't shift gears as you move into your day, you may be tempted to skip writing it down. But even jotting down a summary or outline can help move it out of your head so you can reflect on it later. You can also get moving with a few minutes of brisk exercise such as walking outside, marching in place, dancing, or doing a few rounds of sun salutations to get back into your body and the present moment.

Let placid slumbers sooth each weary mind,

At morn to wake more heav'nly, more refin'd.

Phillis Wheatley,
"A Hymn to the Evening"

help is on the way

It's rare, but sometimes dreams can bring up issues that are challenging to deal with alone. If talking to a friend isn't enough, meet with a psychotherapist, dreamwork professional, spiritual director, or licensed counselor to get the guidance you need.

take care

Working with your dreams is interesting and fun. It's also meaningful and rewarding work. So, use your commitment to dream journaling as a healthy excuse to pamper yourself. Give yourself a foot or hand massage with soothing rose- or lavender-scented lotions, set up a cozy corner where you can sip your favorite morning beverage and write in your journal, step outside and connect with nature, or put on your favorite music. You deserve it!

Healthy
SLEEP

for

SWEET
DREAMS

People are finally waking up to the ways skimping on sleep compromises health including causing increases in ailments from depression to diabetes, heart issues, and Alzheimer's disease, among others.

But there's less awareness of the healthful properties of dreaming, which accounts for about a quarter of the time we spend asleep. Dreams are a natural and healthy by-product of sleep, and while we're dreaming, the body regulates its temperature, balances our emotions, and integrates learning. Also, our brain stores and classifies memories, making them easier for us to access.

But rather than value our time dreaming and paying attention to dream content, too often people write dreams off as bizarre or meaningless. And that's a shame, because studies show that people who work with their dreams enjoy improved relationships, process grief better, navigate life's transitions more smoothly, and can even heal nightmares.

Journaling also contributes to better heart health and improved moods. A regular journaling habit has even been shown to improve sleep, which is an extra boon for dreamers!

Dream journaling combines the healthful benefits of sleep, dreams, and putting pen to paper. The first step is to make bedtime a priority, which is not always easy to do. These seven tips for a good eight (or so) hours of sleep can help. Try adding one or more at a time to your evening routine:

1. set up for sleep

A cool, quiet, dark environment with minimal distractions is optimal for sleep. Set your thermostat to about 65–68 degrees Fahrenheit (18–20 degrees Celsius) and try using a sleep mask and/or earplugs to minimize light and sound if needed.

2. back into bedtime

Plan your evening so you get into bed in time for a good eight hours of quality rest. You can use your journal to observe which habits help or hinder your sleep routine. Then make adjustments accordingly.

3. unplug, literally

Knowing that our devices with screens and plugs interfere with sleep by stimulating our mind and distracting us from healthy habits doesn't make unplugging from them any easier. Try setting an alarm to remind you to put your phones and tablets away about an hour before bedtime. And pledge to make your bedroom a screen-free zone. Try it for a week or month as an experiment and keep recommitting to this pledge if you can. Notice how it helps you to wind down and recharge when you do.

4. relax the body to relax the mind

Ease into bedtime with gentle stretches, dimmed lights, and quiet music. As the body settles down, so will your thoughts.

5. beditate

Add a short meditation just before bed—or meditate in bed, sitting up or lying down, to quiet your mind and prepare for sleep. You can also meditate in the middle of the night if you wake up. Nodding off on a meditation cushion is discouraged, but it's okay to drift into dreams when you meditate in bed.

5. the sleep-stealer between your ears

Stressful thoughts are among the greatest obstacles to sleep. Use your journal, especially the bedtime prompts, to clear your mind before bed.

6. count your blessings

Studies show that people who go to bed focusing on what they're thankful for sleep better. So, rather than counting sheep, list three to ten things you're grateful for before bed. Then, imagine each one as you drift off to the Land of Nod.

7. gather more wool—and dreams

We go through several dream cycles each night, each one stretching longer than the last. That means, most memorable dreams occur in the early morning hours. So, to have more dreams, be sure to get plenty of sleep.

I am a writer, a woman who wants to share her dreams. I am a dreamer, a writer without words.

Tzivia Gover,
Dreaming on the Page

Dream

TYPES

As you write down your dreams, you will notice that while there are endless variations, there are also some key categories that many dreams fall into. It's worth noting that you will likely experience one or more of these five types: Lucid Dreams, Recurring Dreams, Nightmares, Dreams of Death and Dying, and Extraordinary Dreams at some point. You'll find a brief explanation for each one here. You can also add to this list if there's a type of dream you experience that hasn't been included.

lucid

In a lucid dream you are aware that you're dreaming while you are dreaming. While lucid, you can make choices: to do a backflip, fly, or walk through walls, for example. You can also use lucidity to gain insight for personal growth and explore life's big questions.

It can happen spontaneously, but it helps to prepare your sleeping mind to recognize that you're in a dream. Your journal can help: Review your dream reports and underline unusual occurrences that could only happen in a dream. For example, you're drinking tea with a deceased friend, or an apple floats away before you can bite into it. Flag these "only-in-a-dream" moments to train your mind to recognize clues that you're dreaming while you're asleep. When you achieve lucidity, enjoy the ride! Then, write about it.

recurring

Every few months you dream you're in your childhood home. Or night after night you dream you're still with your ex, who you haven't spoken to for ages. No matter what form they take, when dream scenarios or dream images are on repeat there is a message that you're not receiving. Perhaps it's time to get a new perspective on how you're responding to a situation in your life. Or maybe it's an invitation to update an old story or an unhelpful belief about yourself.

Welcome these dreams as learning opportunities. In your journal, ask what recurring belief or pattern your dream is bringing to your attention. Try looking at the situation from different angles and/or script new and affirming beliefs instead.

With time and attention, your recurring dream will fade away. Or it might return with a new twist that clues you into what else this dream has to teach you.

nightmares

When a dream scares you awake with your heart racing, it's natural to resist writing it down. But describing the dream on the page can reveal the helpful messages that even the most frightening dreams contain.

Awake, with pen in hand, you are in control. You can slow down or stop writing at any time. You can also write the dream in the third person (*she*, *he*, or *they* instead of *I*) to create some safe distance. Or experiment with writing better endings for the dream.

When you're ready to face the dream antagonist or the danger in the dream, ask questions like:

> *If I'm being attacked or sabotaged in the dream, is there a way*
> *I'm feeling attacked or sabotaged in waking life?*
> *If I'm running away or hiding in the dream, is there anything*
> *I'm running or hiding from in my life?*

In each case consider emotions, thoughts, and feelings as well as relationships and situations.

> *What might I learn if I dared to confront this?*
> *Is there any guidance being offered from a bystander or other*
> *element in the dream that I may have overlooked?*
> *In what ways might this scenario be prodding me toward*
> *positive growth?*

Turning toward scary dreams is a brave thing to do. It's also rewarding when you can identify the problem that the dream represents so you can take appropriate action. Plus, working with nightmares can decrease their frequency and help you feel more courageous and prepared if they do return. Also try:

1. say what you see

When you wake from an upsetting or frightening dream, bring yourself back to safety by naming the colors you see in your room. Say them out loud: "There's the red chair, the blue cushion, the yellow curtains ..." and so on.

2. use your imagination

Re-dream the scenario while you're awake to neutralize the scary elements. Use your imagination to call on any special powers or helpers such as a protective force-field, a dream doctor, security guard, getaway car, etc., that you need to get your dream-self back to safety.

3. return when you're ready

When you're ready, return to the dream using some of the tips in this journal to find the helpful messages this nightmare might have for you.

dreams of death and dying

Although they might feel deeply unsettling, dreams of death and dying, including dreams of deceased loved ones, are common—and wise. Remember that most dreams speak metaphorically. Death in a dream might represent areas in your life where you need to acknowledge endings and make way for new beginnings.

These dreams also encourage us to approach painful losses with more grace. Or they might be prodding you to resolve unfinished business with someone in your life now, or symbolically with someone who has moved on or passed away.

As you write about a dream involving death, ask yourself: Is it time to confront your fears, prepare for change, or cultivate courage and curiosity in the face of the unknown? Is there a relationship you need to mourn? An old story or unhelpful belief that needs to be buried? What changes can you make to breathe new energy into your life?

extraordinary dreams

Some call them big dreams, dreams of clear light, or memorable dreams. These extraordinary dreams may be accompanied by unearthly light, angelic music, or luminous colors. Some contain information that you couldn't have known on your own. They often deliver spiritual guidance or creative inspirations that can resonate for years, decades, or even a lifetime.

Extraordinary dreams can be so clear and direct that you don't feel like you need to analyze them. But write them down anyway and return to them from time to time. You might discover new information and deeper meaning when you do.

Profound wisdom comes through reflection on dreams. No one has known himself truly who has not studied his dreams.

Swami Sivananda,
Philosophy of Dreams

*The solution of the
secret of our lives lies
in our dreams.*

Frederik van Eeden,
The Bride of Dreams

How to *use* the

DAILY
JOURNAL
PAGES

With the tap of a finger, you can share images, videos, and audio recordings of nearly anything you experience. But even our high-tech gadgets can't bring back so much as a snapshot from a dream. (Though stay tuned—at the pace science is progressing, that might change!)

The dream report is still the best way to keep a record of our ephemeral nightly adventures. The Daily Template provides an effective and efficient way to compose your dream entries.

using the daily template

1. date

Start each entry with the date. This vital but often overlooked bit of information helps you locate dream reports and highlight connections between dreams and daytime experiences. You might even identify instances where a dream scenario manifests in future events.

2. dream title

Give your dream a title as if it is a story, poem, or movie. The title can be straightforward (*Packing for a Trip*) or something more expressive. Don't overthink it. Go with the motto *first thought best thought* on this.

3. in this dream

By now you know the importance of writing down dreams—but how you write them is important, too. These guidelines will help you get the most out of your dream reports:

- Start with the phrase *In this dream* ... and write your dream as if the events are happening now (*I am* ... rather than *I was* ...). This keeps you connected with the energy, emotions, and actions of the dream.
- First, focus on the dream itself, leaving any commentary, editorializing, or associations for later.
- Record the dream in as much sensory detail as you can. Include the colors, movements, the quality of the light, sounds, textures, etc. The more you practice noticing, the more you *will* notice.
- You'd be surprised how difficult it can be later on to distinguish between dream reports or something that happened when you were awake. So, mark the end of your dream report by writing *End of Dream* or the initials *EOD*. You can also draw a crescent moon ☾ to mark the beginning of a dream report, and a sun ☼ to mark the start of an entry about your day.

4. emotion

It can be difficult to say what you were feeling in a dream, but it's important to try. The emotions in your dreams hold energy and information—and they can connect you to the incident that prompted the dream. To get to the root of the feeling, try pinpointing one of the four basic emotions: *Mad*, *Sad*, *Glad*, or *Afraid*. There's also space to include other emotions as well.

5. this dream is telling me ...

After you've spent some time with your dream, consider the phrase *This dream may be telling me ...* Continue the sentence with the first thought that comes to mind. There are no wrong answers, and as soon as you consider the prompt, you've opened a channel for wisdom to flow in—either now or later on.

6. quick draw

Dreams are rich in imagery, so take a minute (or less!) to sketch an element of your dream in the space provided. Drawing the dream reveals new aspects, helps with recall, and it's fun. No artistic talent is necessary: stick figures and basic shapes work just fine here.

7. action step

To supercharge your dream's healing potential, create a brief affirmation, motto, or action statement based on it. Complete this sentence: *In response to this dream, today I will ...*

8. bedtime prompts

This is a space to put your day to bed before you turn off the light. Here, you will reflect on what you did and clear worries from your mind as you prepare for sweet sleep and dreams.

DREAM TITLE: DATE:
_____

In this dream ...
....
....
....
....
....
....
....
....
....
....
....
....
....
....
....
....
....
....

I felt (circle one):   MAD   SAD   GLAD   AFRAID

I also felt ...
....
This dream may be telling me ...
....
....
....

QUICK DRAW

ACTION STEP

In response to this dream, today I will ...

BEDTIME PROMPTS

Three things I did:

☆

☆

☆

Something I felt:

Three things I'm grateful for:

☆

☆

☆

Something I'm worried about:

DREAM TITLE: **DATE:**

In this dream ...

I felt (circle one):   MAD   SAD   GLAD   AFRAID

I also felt ...

This dream may be telling me ...

QUICK DRAW

ACTION STEP

In response to this dream, today I will ...

....

....

....

BEDTIME PROMPTS

Three things I did:

☆ ....

☆ ....

☆ ....

Something I felt:

....

....

Three things I'm grateful for:

☆ ....

☆ ....

☆ ....

Something I'm worried about:

....

....

DREAM TITLE: **DATE:**

In this dream …

I felt (circle one):   MAD   SAD   GLAD   AFRAID

I also felt …

This dream may be telling me …

QUICK DRAW

ACTION STEP

In response to this dream, today I will ...

....

....

....

BEDTIME PROMPTS

Three things I did:

☆
....

☆
....

☆
....

Something I felt:

....

....

Three things I'm grateful for:

☆
....

☆
....

☆
....

Something I'm worried about:

....

....

DREAM TITLE: **DATE:**

In this dream ...

I felt (circle one):   MAD   SAD   GLAD   AFRAID

I also felt ...

This dream may be telling me ...

QUICK DRAW

ACTION STEP

In response to this dream, today I will ...

BEDTIME PROMPTS

Three things I did:

☆

☆

☆

Something I felt:

Three things I'm grateful for:

☆

☆

☆

Something I'm worried about:

DREAM TITLE: **DATE:**

In this dream ...

I felt (circle one):   MAD   SAD   GLAD   AFRAID

I also felt ...

This dream may be telling me ...

QUICK DRAW

ACTION STEP

In response to this dream, today I will ...

BEDTIME PROMPTS

Three things I did:

☆

☆

☆

Something I felt:

Three things I'm grateful for:

☆

☆

☆

Something I'm worried about:

DREAM TITLE: **DATE:**

In this dream ...

I felt (circle one):   MAD   SAD   GLAD   AFRAID

I also felt ...

This dream may be telling me ...

QUICK DRAW

ACTION STEP

In response to this dream, today I will ...

BEDTIME PROMPTS

Three things I did:

☆

☆

☆

Something I felt:

Three things I'm grateful for:

☆

☆

☆

Something I'm worried about:

DREAM TITLE: **DATE:**

In this dream ...

I felt (circle one):   MAD   SAD   GLAD   AFRAID

I also felt ...

This dream may be telling me ...

56

QUICK DRAW

ACTION STEP

In response to this dream, today I will ...

....

....

....

BEDTIME PROMPTS

Three things I did: *Three things I'm grateful for:*

☆   ☆
....

☆   ☆
....

☆   ☆
....

Something I felt: *Something I'm worried about:*

....

....

DREAM TITLE: **DATE:**

In this dream ...

I felt (circle one):   MAD   SAD   GLAD   AFRAID

I also felt ...

This dream may be telling me ...

QUICK DRAW

ACTION STEP

In response to this dream, today I will …

BEDTIME PROMPTS

Three things I did:

☆

☆

☆

Something I felt:

Three things I'm grateful for:

☆

☆

☆

Something I'm worried about:

DREAM TITLE: **DATE:**

In this dream ...

I felt (circle one):   MAD   SAD   GLAD   AFRAID

I also felt ...

This dream may be telling me ...

QUICK DRAW

ACTION STEP

In response to this dream, today I will ...

....

....

....

BEDTIME PROMPTS

Three things I did:

☆ ....

☆ ....

☆ ....

Something I felt:

....

....

Three things I'm grateful for:

☆ ....

☆ ....

☆ ....

Something I'm worried about:

....

....

DREAM TITLE: **DATE:**

In this dream ...

....

....

....

....

....

....

....

....

....

....

....

....

....

....

....

....

....

....

....

....

I felt (circle one):   MAD   SAD   GLAD   AFRAID

I also felt ...

This dream may be telling me ...

....

....

....

QUICK DRAW

ACTION STEP

In response to this dream, today I will ...

BEDTIME PROMPTS

Three things I did:

☆

☆

☆

Something I felt:

Three things I'm grateful for:

☆

☆

☆

Something I'm worried about:

DREAM TITLE: **DATE:**

In this dream ...

I felt (circle one):   MAD   SAD   GLAD   AFRAID

I also felt ...

This dream may be telling me ...

QUICK DRAW

ACTION STEP

In response to this dream, today I will ...

BEDTIME PROMPTS

Three things I did:

☆

☆

☆

Something I felt:

Three things I'm grateful for:

☆

☆

☆

Something I'm worried about:

DREAM TITLE: **DATE:**

In this dream ...

I felt (circle one):   MAD   SAD   GLAD   AFRAID

I also felt ...

This dream may be telling me ...

QUICK DRAW

ACTION STEP

In response to this dream, today I will ...

BEDTIME PROMPTS

Three things I did:

☆

☆

☆

Something I felt:

Three things I'm grateful for:

☆

☆

☆

Something I'm worried about:

DREAM TITLE: DATE:

In this dream ...

I felt (circle one): MAD SAD GLAD AFRAID

I also felt ...

This dream may be telling me ...

QUICK DRAW

ACTION STEP

In response to this dream, today I will ...

BEDTIME PROMPTS

Three things I did:

☆

☆

☆

Something I felt:

Three things I'm grateful for:

☆

☆

☆

Something I'm worried about:

DREAM TITLE: **DATE:**

In this dream ...

I felt (circle one):   MAD   SAD   GLAD   AFRAID

I also felt ...

This dream may be telling me ...

QUICK DRAW

ACTION STEP

In response to this dream, today I will ...

BEDTIME PROMPTS

Three things I did:

☆

☆

☆

Something I felt:

Three things I'm grateful for:

☆

☆

☆

Something I'm worried about:

DREAM TITLE: **DATE:**

In this dream ...

I felt (circle one):   MAD   SAD   GLAD   AFRAID

I also felt ...

This dream may be telling me ...

QUICK DRAW

ACTION STEP

In response to this dream, today I will ...

BEDTIME PROMPTS

Three things I did:

☆
☆
☆

Something I felt:

Three things I'm grateful for:

☆
☆
☆

Something I'm worried about:

DREAM TITLE: **DATE:**

In this dream ...

I felt (circle one):   MAD   SAD   GLAD   AFRAID

I also felt ...

This dream may be telling me ...

QUICK DRAW

ACTION STEP

In response to this dream, today I will ...

BEDTIME PROMPTS

Three things I did:

☆

☆

☆

Something I felt:

Three things I'm grateful for:

☆

☆

☆

Something I'm worried about:

DREAM TITLE: **DATE:**

In this dream ...

I felt (circle one):   MAD   SAD   GLAD   AFRAID

I also felt ...

This dream may be telling me ...

QUICK DRAW

ACTION STEP

In response to this dream, today I will ...

BEDTIME PROMPTS

Three things I did:

☆

☆

☆

Something I felt:

Three things I'm grateful for:

☆

☆

☆

Something I'm worried about:

DREAM TITLE: **DATE:**

In this dream ...

I felt (circle one):   MAD   SAD   GLAD   AFRAID

I also felt ...

This dream may be telling me ...

QUICK DRAW

ACTION STEP

In response to this dream, today I will ...

....

....

....

BEDTIME PROMPTS

Three things I did: *Three things I'm grateful for:*

☆   ☆
....

☆   ☆
....

☆   ☆
....

Something I felt: *Something I'm worried about:*

....

....

DREAM TITLE: DATE:

In this dream ...

I felt (circle one):   MAD   SAD   GLAD   AFRAID

I also felt ...

This dream may be telling me ...

QUICK DRAW

ACTION STEP

In response to this dream, today I will ...

BEDTIME PROMPTS

Three things I did:

☆
☆
☆

Something I felt:

Three things I'm grateful for:

☆
☆
☆

Something I'm worried about:

DREAM TITLE: DATE:

In this dream ...

I felt (circle one): MAD SAD GLAD AFRAID

I also felt ...

This dream may be telling me ...

QUICK DRAW

ACTION STEP

In response to this dream, today I will ...

BEDTIME PROMPTS

Three things I did:

☆

☆

☆

Something I felt:

Three things I'm grateful for:

☆

☆

☆

Something I'm worried about:

DREAM TITLE: **DATE:**

In this dream ...

I felt (circle one):   MAD   SAD   GLAD   AFRAID

I also felt ...

This dream may be telling me ...

QUICK DRAW

ACTION STEP

In response to this dream, today I will ...

BEDTIME PROMPTS

Three things I did:

☆

☆

☆

Something I felt:

Three things I'm grateful for:

☆

☆

☆

Something I'm worried about:

DREAM TITLE: **DATE:**

In this dream ...

I felt (circle one):   MAD   SAD   GLAD   AFRAID

I also felt ...

This dream may be telling me ...

QUICK DRAW

ACTION STEP

In response to this dream, today I will ...

BEDTIME PROMPTS

Three things I did:

☆

☆

☆

Something I felt:

Three things I'm grateful for:

☆

A

☆

Something I'm worried about:

DREAM TITLE: **DATE:**

In this dream ...

I felt (circle one):   MAD   SAD   GLAD   AFRAID

I also felt ...

This dream may be telling me ...

QUICK DRAW

ACTION STEP

In response to this dream, today I will ...

....

....

....

BEDTIME PROMPTS

Three things I did:

☆ ....

☆ ....

☆ ....

Something I felt:

....

....

Three things I'm grateful for:

☆ ....

☆ ....

☆ ....

Something I'm worried about:

....

....

DREAM TITLE: DATE:

In this dream ...

I felt (circle one): MAD SAD GLAD AFRAID

I also felt ...

This dream may be telling me ...

QUICK DRAW

ACTION STEP

In response to this dream, today I will ...

....

....

....

BEDTIME PROMPTS

Three things I did: *Three things I'm grateful for:*

☆   ☆
....

☆   ☆
....

☆   ☆
....

Something I felt: *Something I'm worried about:*

....

....

DREAM TITLE: **DATE:**

In this dream ...

I felt (circle one):   MAD   SAD   GLAD   AFRAID

I also felt ...

This dream may be telling me ...

QUICK DRAW

ACTION STEP

In response to this dream, today I will ...

BEDTIME PROMPTS

Three things I did:

☆

☆

☆

Something I felt:

Three things I'm grateful for:

☆

☆

☆

Something I'm worried about:

DREAM TITLE: **DATE:**

In this dream ...

I felt (circle one):   MAD   SAD   GLAD   AFRAID

I also felt ...

This dream may be telling me ...

QUICK DRAW

ACTION STEP

In response to this dream, today I will ...
....
....
....

BEDTIME PROMPTS

Three things I did:

☆ ....

☆ ....

☆ ....

Something I felt:

....

....

Three things I'm grateful for:

☆ ....

☆ ....

☆ ....

Something I'm worried about:

....

....

DREAM TITLE: **DATE:**

In this dream ...

I felt (circle one):   MAD   SAD   GLAD   AFRAID

I also felt ...

This dream may be telling me ...

QUICK DRAW

ACTION STEP

In response to this dream, today I will ...

BEDTIME PROMPTS

Three things I did:

☆

☆

☆

Something I felt:

Three things I'm grateful for:

☆

☆

☆

Something I'm worried about:

DREAM TITLE: **DATE:**

In this dream ...

I felt (circle one):   MAD   SAD   GLAD   AFRAID

I also felt ...

This dream may be telling me ...

QUICK DRAW

ACTION STEP

In response to this dream, today I will ...

BEDTIME PROMPTS

Three things I did:

☆

☆

☆

Three things I'm grateful for:

☆

☆

☆

Something I felt:

Something I'm worried about:

DREAM TITLE: **DATE:**

In this dream ...

I felt (circle one):   MAD   SAD   GLAD   AFRAID

I also felt ...

This dream may be telling me ...

QUICK DRAW

ACTION STEP

In response to this dream, today I will ...

BEDTIME PROMPTS

Three things I did:

☆

☆

☆

Something I felt:

Three things I'm grateful for:

☆

☆

☆

Something I'm worried about:

DREAM TITLE: **DATE:**

In this dream ...

I felt (circle one):   MAD   SAD   GLAD   AFRAID

I also felt ...

This dream may be telling me ...

QUICK DRAW

ACTION STEP

In response to this dream, today I will ...

BEDTIME PROMPTS

Three things I did:

☆

☆

☆

Something I felt:

Three things I'm grateful for:

☆

☆

☆

Something I'm worried about:

DREAM TITLE: _____ **DATE:** _____

In this dream ...

_____

_____

_____

_____

_____

_____

_____

_____

_____

_____

_____

_____

_____

_____

_____

_____

_____

_____

_____

I felt (circle one):   MAD   SAD   GLAD   AFRAID

I also felt ...

This dream may be telling me ...

_____

_____

_____

QUICK DRAW

ACTION STEP

In response to this dream, today I will ...

BEDTIME PROMPTS

Three things I did:

☆

☆

☆

Something I felt:

Three things I'm grateful for:

☆

☆

☆

Something I'm worried about:

DREAM TITLE: DATE:

In this dream ...

I felt (circle one): MAD SAD GLAD AFRAID

I also felt ...

This dream may be telling me ...

QUICK DRAW

ACTION STEP

In response to this dream, today I will ...

....

....

....

BEDTIME PROMPTS

Three things I did:

☆

☆

☆

Something I felt:

Three things I'm grateful for:

☆

☆

☆

Something I'm worried about:

DREAM TITLE: **DATE:**

In this dream ...

I felt (circle one):   MAD   SAD   GLAD   AFRAID

I also felt ...

This dream may be telling me ...

QUICK DRAW

ACTION STEP

In response to this dream, today I will ...
....
....
....

BEDTIME PROMPTS

Three things I did:

☆
....

☆
....

☆
....

Something I felt:

....

....

Three things I'm grateful for:

☆
....

☆
....

☆
....

Something I'm worried about:

....

....

DREAM TITLE: **DATE:**

In this dream ...

I felt (circle one):   MAD   SAD   GLAD   AFRAID

I also felt ...

This dream may be telling me ...

QUICK DRAW

ACTION STEP

In response to this dream, today I will ...

BEDTIME PROMPTS

Three things I did:

☆

☆

☆

Something I felt:

Three things I'm grateful for:

☆

☆

☆

Something I'm worried about:

DREAM TITLE: **DATE:**

In this dream ...

I felt (circle one):   MAD   SAD   GLAD   AFRAID

I also felt ...

This dream may be telling me ...

QUICK DRAW

ACTION STEP

In response to this dream, today I will ...

BEDTIME PROMPTS

Three things I did:

☆

☆

☆

Something I felt:

Three things I'm grateful for:

☆

☆

☆

Something I'm worried about:

DREAM TITLE: **DATE:**

In this dream ...

I felt (circle one):   MAD   SAD   GLAD   AFRAID

I also felt ...

This dream may be telling me ...

QUICK DRAW

ACTION STEP

In response to this dream, today I will ...

BEDTIME PROMPTS

Three things I did:

☆

☆

☆

Something I felt:

Three things I'm grateful for:

☆

☆

☆

Something I'm worried about:

DREAM TITLE: **DATE:**

In this dream ...

I felt (circle one):   MAD   SAD   GLAD   AFRAID

I also felt ...

This dream may be telling me ...

QUICK DRAW

ACTION STEP

In response to this dream, today I will ...

BEDTIME PROMPTS

Three things I did:

☆

☆

☆

Something I felt:

Three things I'm grateful for:

☆

☆

☆

Something I'm worried about:

DREAM TITLE: **DATE:**

In this dream ...

I felt (circle one):   MAD   SAD   GLAD   AFRAID

I also felt ...

This dream may be telling me ...

QUICK DRAW

ACTION STEP

In response to this dream, today I will ...

BEDTIME PROMPTS

Three things I did:

☆

☆

☆

Something I felt:

Three things I'm grateful for:

☆

☆

☆

Something I'm worried about:

DREAM TITLE: **DATE:**

In this dream ...

I felt (circle one):   MAD   SAD   GLAD   AFRAID

I also felt ...

This dream may be telling me ...

QUICK DRAW

ACTION STEP

In response to this dream, today I will ...

BEDTIME PROMPTS

Three things I did:

☆

☆

☆

Something I felt:

Three things I'm grateful for:

☆

☆

☆

Something I'm worried about:

DREAM TITLE: **DATE:**

In this dream ...

_____

_____

_____

_____

_____

_____

_____

_____

_____

_____

_____

_____

_____

_____

_____

_____

_____

_____

_____

I felt (circle one):   MAD   SAD   GLAD   AFRAID

I also felt ...

This dream may be telling me ...

_____

_____

_____

QUICK DRAW

ACTION STEP

In response to this dream, today I will ...

BEDTIME PROMPTS

Three things I did:

☆

☆

☆

Something I felt:

Three things I'm grateful for:

☆

☆

☆

Something I'm worried about:

DREAM TITLE: **DATE:**

In this dream ...

_____

_____

_____

_____

_____

_____

_____

_____

_____

_____

_____

_____

_____

_____

_____

_____

_____

I felt (circle one):   MAD   SAD   GLAD   AFRAID

I also felt ...

This dream may be telling me ...

_____

_____

QUICK DRAW

ACTION STEP

In response to this dream, today I will ...

....

....

....

BEDTIME PROMPTS

Three things I did:

☆

....

☆

....

☆

....

Something I felt:

....

....

Three things I'm grateful for:

☆

....

☆

....

☆

....

Something I'm worried about:

....

....

DREAM TITLE: **DATE:**

In this dream ...

I felt (circle one):   MAD   SAD   GLAD   AFRAID

I also felt ...

This dream may be telling me ...

QUICK DRAW

ACTION STEP

In response to this dream, today I will ...

BEDTIME PROMPTS

Three things I did:

☆

☆

☆

Something I felt:

Three things I'm grateful for:

☆

☆

☆

Something I'm worried about:

DREAM TITLE: **DATE:**

In this dream ...

I felt (circle one):   MAD   SAD   GLAD   AFRAID

I also felt ...

This dream may be telling me ...

QUICK DRAW

ACTION STEP

In response to this dream, today I will ...

BEDTIME PROMPTS

Three things I did:

☆

☆

☆

Something I felt:

Three things I'm grateful for:

☆

☆

☆

Something I'm worried about:

DREAM TITLE: **DATE:**

In this dream ...

I felt (circle one):   MAD   SAD   GLAD   AFRAID

I also felt ...

This dream may be telling me ...

QUICK DRAW

ACTION STEP

In response to this dream, today I will ...

BEDTIME PROMPTS

Three things I did:

☆

☆

☆

Something I felt:

Three things I'm grateful for:

☆

☆

☆

Something I'm worried about:

DREAM TITLE: **DATE:**

In this dream ...

I felt (circle one):   MAD   SAD   GLAD   AFRAID

I also felt ...

This dream may be telling me ...

QUICK DRAW

ACTION STEP

In response to this dream, today I will ...

BEDTIME PROMPTS

Three things I did:

☆

☆

☆

Something I felt:

Three things I'm grateful for:

☆

☆

☆

Something I'm worried about:

DREAM TITLE: **DATE:**

In this dream ...

I felt (circle one):   MAD   SAD   GLAD   AFRAID

I also felt ...

This dream may be telling me ...

QUICK DRAW

ACTION STEP

In response to this dream, today I will ...

BEDTIME PROMPTS

Three things I did:

☆

☆

☆

Something I felt:

Three things I'm grateful for:

☆

☆

☆

Something I'm worried about:

DREAM TITLE: **DATE:**

In this dream ...

I felt (circle one):   MAD   SAD   GLAD   AFRAID

I also felt ...

This dream may be telling me ...

QUICK DRAW

ACTION STEP

In response to this dream, today I will ...

BEDTIME PROMPTS

Three things I did:

☆

☆

☆

Something I felt:

Three things I'm grateful for:

☆

☆

☆

Something I'm worried about:

DREAM TITLE: **DATE:**

In this dream ...

I felt (circle one):   MAD   SAD   GLAD   AFRAID

I also felt ...

This dream may be telling me ...

QUICK DRAW

ACTION STEP

In response to this dream, today I will ...

BEDTIME PROMPTS

Three things I did:

☆

☆

☆

Something I felt:

Three things I'm grateful for:

☆

☆

☆

Something I'm worried about:

DREAM TITLE: **DATE:**

In this dream ...

I felt (circle one):   MAD   SAD   GLAD   AFRAID

I also felt ...

This dream may be telling me ...

QUICK DRAW

ACTION STEP

In response to this dream, today I will ...

BEDTIME PROMPTS

Three things I did:

☆

☆

☆

Something I felt:

Three things I'm grateful for:

☆

☆

☆

Something I'm worried about:

DREAM TITLE: **DATE:**

In this dream ...

I felt (circle one):   MAD   SAD   GLAD   AFRAID

I also felt ...

This dream may be telling me ...

QUICK DRAW

ACTION STEP

In response to this dream, today I will ...

BEDTIME PROMPTS

Three things I did:

☆

☆

☆

Something I felt:

Three things I'm grateful for:

☆

☆

☆

Something I'm worried about:

DREAM TITLE: **DATE:**

In this dream ...

_____

_____

_____

_____

_____

_____

_____

_____

_____

_____

_____

_____

_____

_____

_____

_____

_____

_____

_____

I felt (circle one):   MAD   SAD   GLAD   AFRAID

I also felt ...

This dream may be telling me ...

_____

_____

_____

QUICK DRAW

ACTION STEP

In response to this dream, today I will ...

....

....

....

BEDTIME PROMPTS

Three things I did:

☆

....

☆

....

☆

....

Something I felt:

....

....

Three things I'm grateful for:

☆

....

☆

....

☆

....

Something I'm worried about:

....

....

DREAM TITLE: **DATE:**

In this dream ...

I felt (circle one):   MAD   SAD   GLAD   AFRAID

I also felt ...

This dream may be telling me ...

QUICK DRAW

ACTION STEP

In response to this dream, today I will ...

BEDTIME PROMPTS

Three things I did:

☆

☆

☆

Something I felt:

Three things I'm grateful for:

☆

☆

☆

Something I'm worried about:

DREAM TITLE: DATE:

In this dream ...

I felt (circle one):   MAD   SAD   GLAD   AFRAID

I also felt ...

This dream may be telling me ...

QUICK DRAW

ACTION STEP

In response to this dream, today I will ...

BEDTIME PROMPTS

Three things I did:

☆

☆

☆

Something I felt:

Three things I'm grateful for:

☆

☆

☆

Something I'm worried about:

DREAM TITLE: **DATE:**

In this dream ...

I felt (circle one):   MAD   SAD   GLAD   AFRAID

I also felt ...

This dream may be telling me ...

QUICK DRAW

ACTION STEP

In response to this dream, today I will ...

BEDTIME PROMPTS

Three things I did:

☆

☆

☆

Something I felt:

Three things I'm grateful for:

☆

☆

☆

Something I'm worried about:

DREAM TITLE: **DATE:**

In this dream ...

I felt (circle one):   MAD   SAD   GLAD   AFRAID

I also felt ...

This dream may be telling me ...

QUICK DRAW

ACTION STEP

In response to this dream, today I will ...

....

....

....

BEDTIME PROMPTS

Three things I did: *Three things I'm grateful for:*

☆ ....   ☆ ....

☆ ....   ☆ ....

☆ ....   ☆ ....

Something I felt: *Something I'm worried about:*

....

....

JOURNALING
prompts

Use the lined long-form pages and unlined free-form pages that follow, along with these prompts, to deepen your dreamwork, spark creativity, and unlock more of the meaning and messages in your dreams. Use the prompts that inspire you and tweak or skip those that don't. Add your own if you like, too!

seeing in the dark

When we close our physical eyes and sleep, our inner sight opens onto a whole new world. Appreciate and investigate the imagery of your dreaming mind by making a list of all the things you see in the dream. Zoom in close to take in the smallest details then zoom out and take in the sweeping panorama. It's optional to start each line with the phrase: *With eyes closed, I see …*

let the image speak

Write a story or poem from the perspective of one of the inanimate objects in your dream. When you're done, read it over. What resonates with you?

interview a stranger

Write a dialogue with an unknown person from your dream. Ask them who they are, what they do, what they know that you don't, and what message they have come to bring you.

who was that?

Write down the first three words that come to mind in relation to a person in your dream. Then add three ways this person is most different from you, and three ways they are most similar. What do they know or have that you need for yourself? Now, consider which part of yourself this person might represent. Write about it.

make it mythic

Write a dream as if it's a fairytale or myth. Begin with the words, *Once upon a time* ..., and keep writing.

animal dreams

Write about an animal you encountered in a dream. In addition to a general description, also include three things the animal is doing, two things it is hungry for, and end by imagining what this animal dreams of.

in sync

If you've ever dreamed of someone you haven't seen for ages and then bump into them the next day, you've experienced a synchronicity. This type of coincidence, which connects dreams with waking experiences, tends to occur more often the more you tune in to your dreams. Notice, and when synchronicities pop up, write about them!

wax poetic

Rewrite your dream as if it's a poem. Replace vague words with words that conjure up something more specific. (Instead of *It was beautiful*, you might try *The sky was sapphire blue*.) Write your dream in short or long lines, not because of where a sentence ends, but based on the sounds of the words, or where you want to leave extra space on the page. Go with your gut—and make it poetic!

turn a nightmare into a thriller

Write a scary dream in the third person (*she/he/they* instead of *I*) to gain some distance and reveal the whole story the dream is telling.

gather your dream lines

Page through your journal and copy out some of your favorite sentences or phrases. Then, use the words you've collected to write a five- to fifteen-line poem. It's optional to begin each line with the phrase: *I dream of.*

where it's at

Notice where your dream took place: At a school, a shopping mall, a football field ... Then, consider the purpose or function of this place. Write about it starting with the phrase, *I am in a place of* ... Include plenty of details and description—and keep writing.

happy dream day to you

Special occasions, such as birthdays, New Year's, or the first day of a new job or semester, are ideal times to turn to dreams for guidance. In your journal, pose a question or make a request on the eve of a special event. Ask your dreams to show you what you need to know as you enter this new phase. In the morning create an affirmation or motto that sums up your dream's best wishes for you.

look for the helper

Scan your dream for the element or character that offers the relief or healing you need. Look carefully! Help can appear in unexpected forms, such as a flourishing green plant, the exit ramp on a highway, or a bystander wearing a nurse's uniform, for example. When you find the helper, write about it. What type of assistance can it offer, both in the dream and in your waking life?

becoming whole

Dreams help us find balance and achieve wholeness. Consider where your dream might be showing that you're off kilter (such as too busy, regretful, or passive). Maybe it's prompting you to consider an aspect of yourself you've been neglecting. Complete this sentence: *In order to be more healthy, whole, and complete, my dream may be suggesting* ...

create your own dream prompt

Write some of your dream titles or favorite dream images on slips of paper and place them in a special box or bowl. Select one at random and use it as a writing prompt.

*Just writing your dream
can spark an 'aha!'—that
moment of insight when
you understand what your
dream may have been
trying to tell you.*

Tzivia Gover

An uninterpreted dream
is like an unread letter.

Rav Hisda

Dream
INDEX

In addition to considering individual dreams, it can be beneficial to consider dreams collectively. The Dream Index will help you:

- Find a specific dream report by matching a dream title to the date it was recorded in your journal.

- Identify your most frequent dream images, dream themes, dream emotions, etc.

- Get a snapshot of your dream patterns, frequency of dream recall, and dream types—or anything else you want to track.

As the column headings suggest, you'll take note of the **Date** and **Title** for each dream, and dream **Images**, **Characters**, and **Dream Types** (recurring dreams, nightmares, lucid dreams, extraordinary dreams, etc.). In the **Notes** column you can track anything else that interests you such as dream locations, themes, or the appearance of animals, music, writing, weather, etc.

Two sample entries have been provided to show you how the index can be used.

Fill in the index as you go or make it a monthly or seasonal task. Choose the frequency that works for you.

DATE:	DREAM TITLE:	IMAGE(S):
January 1	*Baby on the beach*	*Sand pail*
		Tidal wave
January 6	*Allie's journal*	*Pages from an*
		artistic journal
		Stars

CHARACTER(S):	DREAM TYPE:	NOTES:
Baby	Recurring	Unlike in other tidal
Lifeguard	(tidal wave)	wave dreams, I felt safe
		in this one.
Allie	Lucid: Halfway through	A particularly colorful
Allie's son	the dream, I knew I	dream, the journal
	was dreaming	pages had gold accents.

DATE:	DREAM TITLE:	IMAGE(S):

CHARACTER(S):	DREAM TYPE:	NOTES:

DATE:	DREAM TITLE:	IMAGE(S):

CHARACTER(S):	DREAM TYPE:	NOTES:

DATE:	DREAM TITLE:	IMAGE(S):

CHARACTER(S):	DREAM TYPE:	NOTES:

Smith Street Books

Published in 2025 by Smith Street Books
Naarm (Melbourne) | Australia
smithstreetbooks.com

ISBN: 978-1-9230-4984-0

Smith Street Books respectfully acknowledges the Wurundjeri People of the Kulin Nation, who are the Traditional Owners of the land on which we work, and we pay our respects to their Elders past and present.

Publisher: Paul McNally
Managing editor: Lucy Heaver
Editor: Sophie Dougall
Designer: Vanessa Masci
Proofreader: Pamela Dunne
Production manager: Aisling Coughlan

Printed & bound in China by C&C Offset Printing Co., Ltd.

Book 375

10 9 8 7 6 5 4 3 2 1

MIX
Paper | Supporting
responsible forestry
FSC® C008047
FSC
www.fsc.org

Tzivia Gover is the author of several books including *Dreaming on the Page*, *The Mindful Way to a Good Night's Sleep*, and *The Little Deck of Dreams*. She offers workshops internationally, domestically, and online, as well as keynotes and classes about dreams, mindfulness, and writing. Tzivia is an executive board member of the International Association for the Study of Dreams, and she has served as the education director for the Institute for Dream Studies. She is a Certified Dreamwork Professional, a Certified Proprioceptive Writing instructor, and she received an MFA in writing from Columbia University. She writes and dreams in western Massachusetts.

Learn more at thirdhousemoon.com.